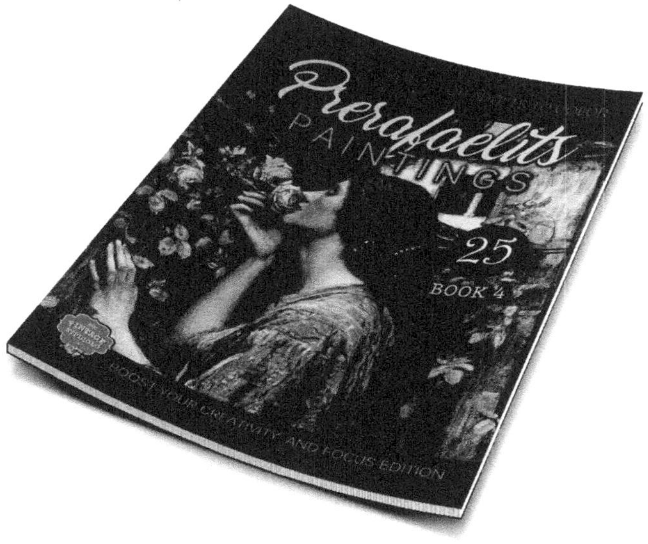

Gray Scale Photos for Adults to Color

Prerafaelits PAINTINGS

BOOK 4

BOOST YOUR CREATIVITY AND FOCUS EDITION

This Book Belongs to

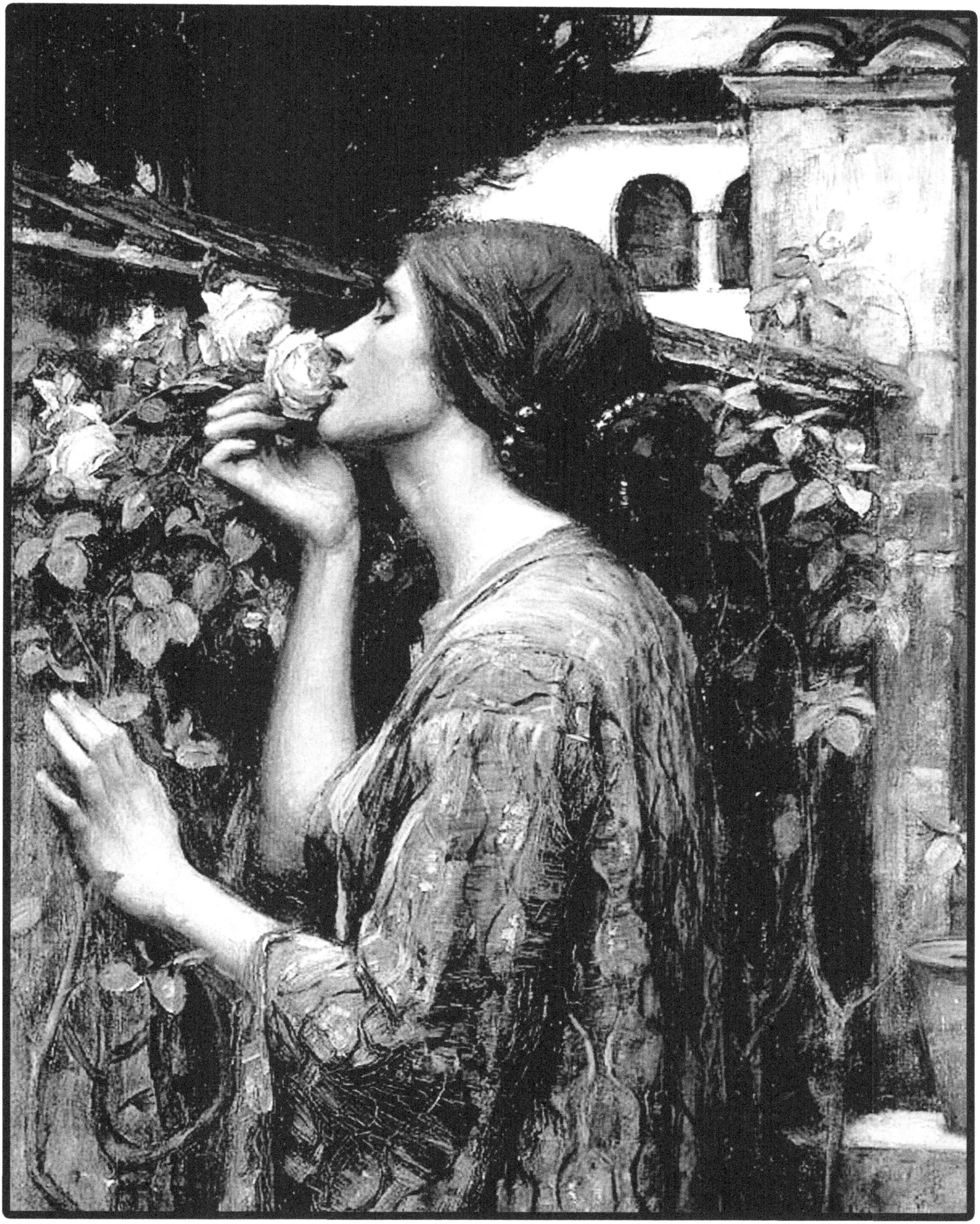

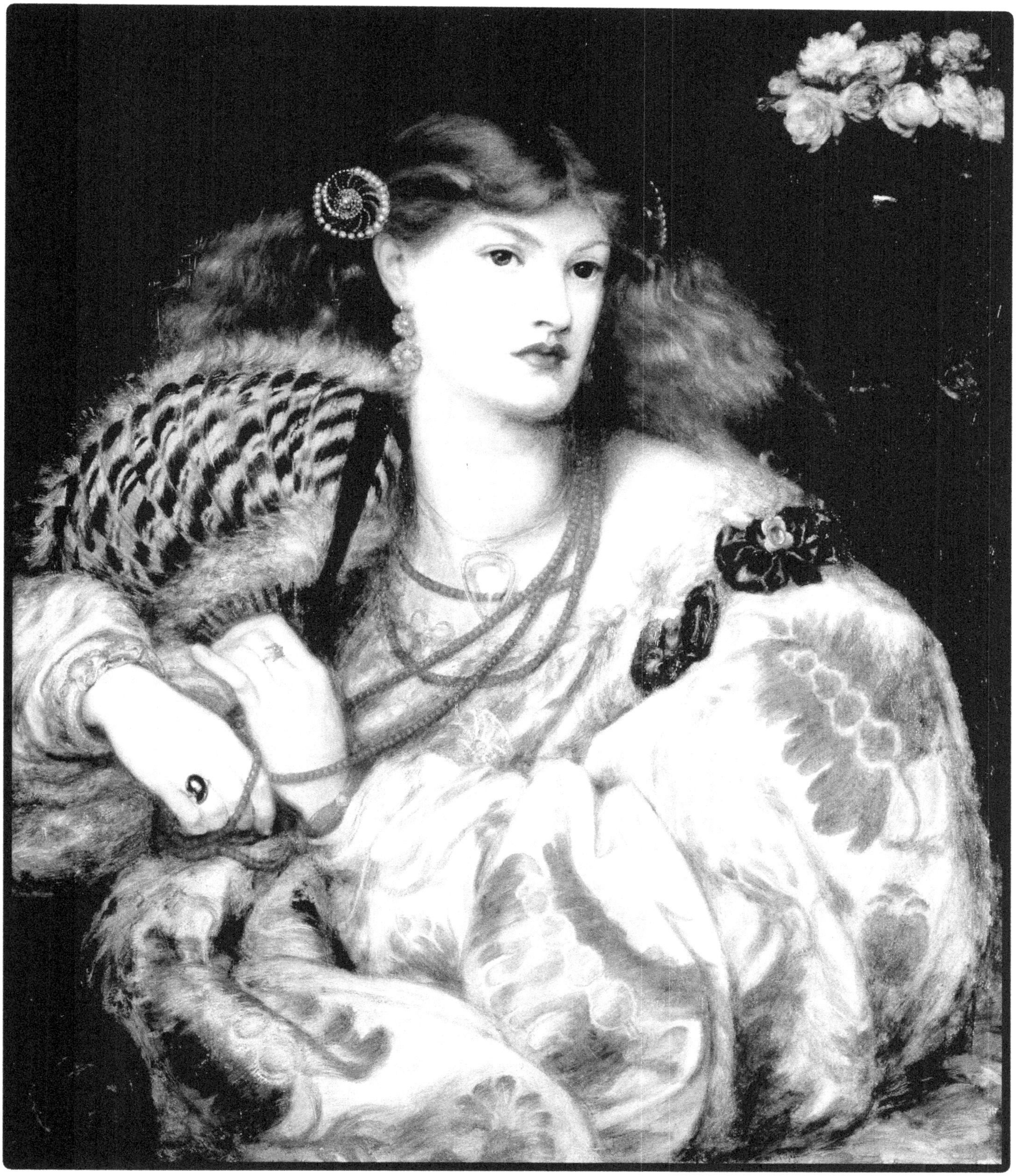

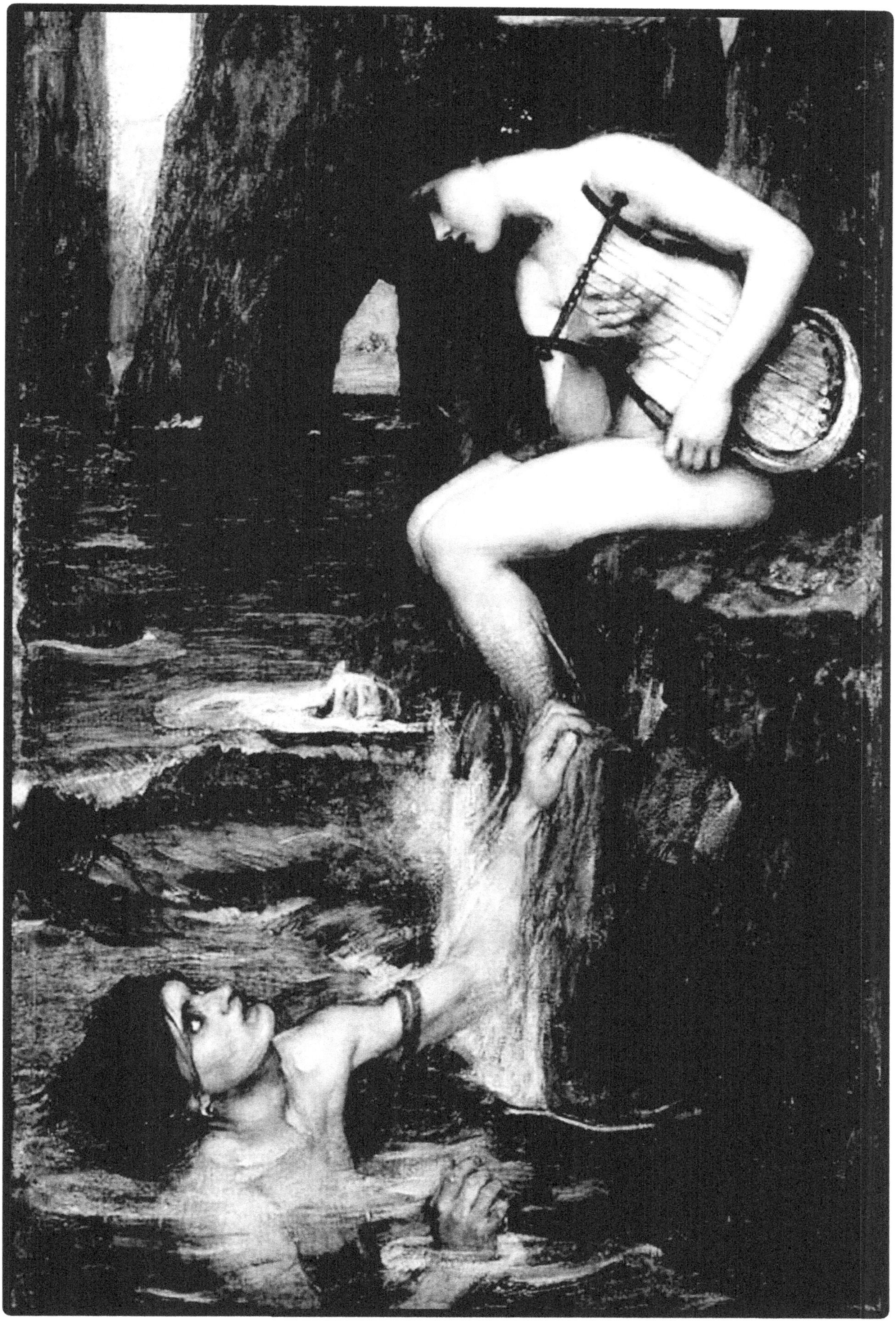

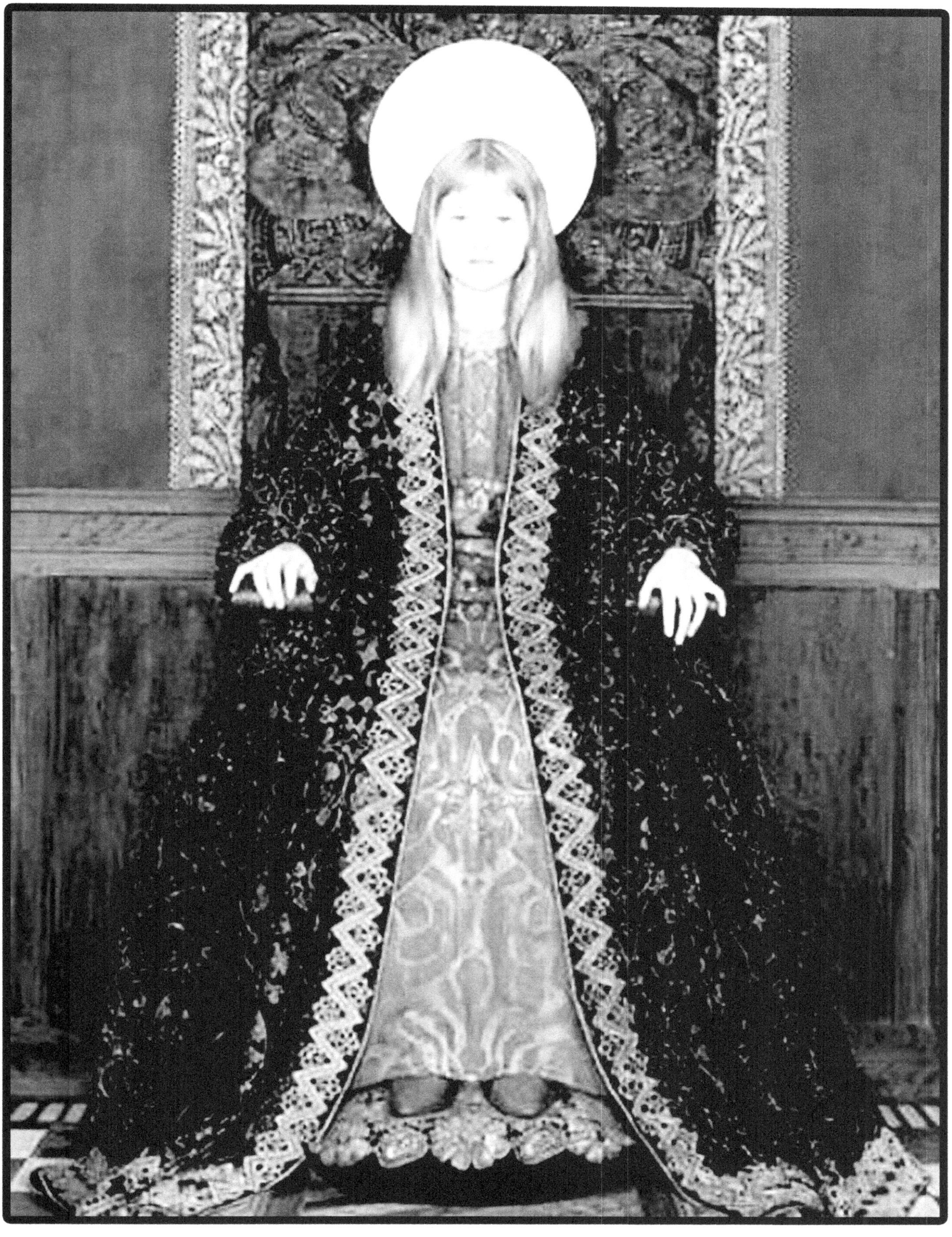

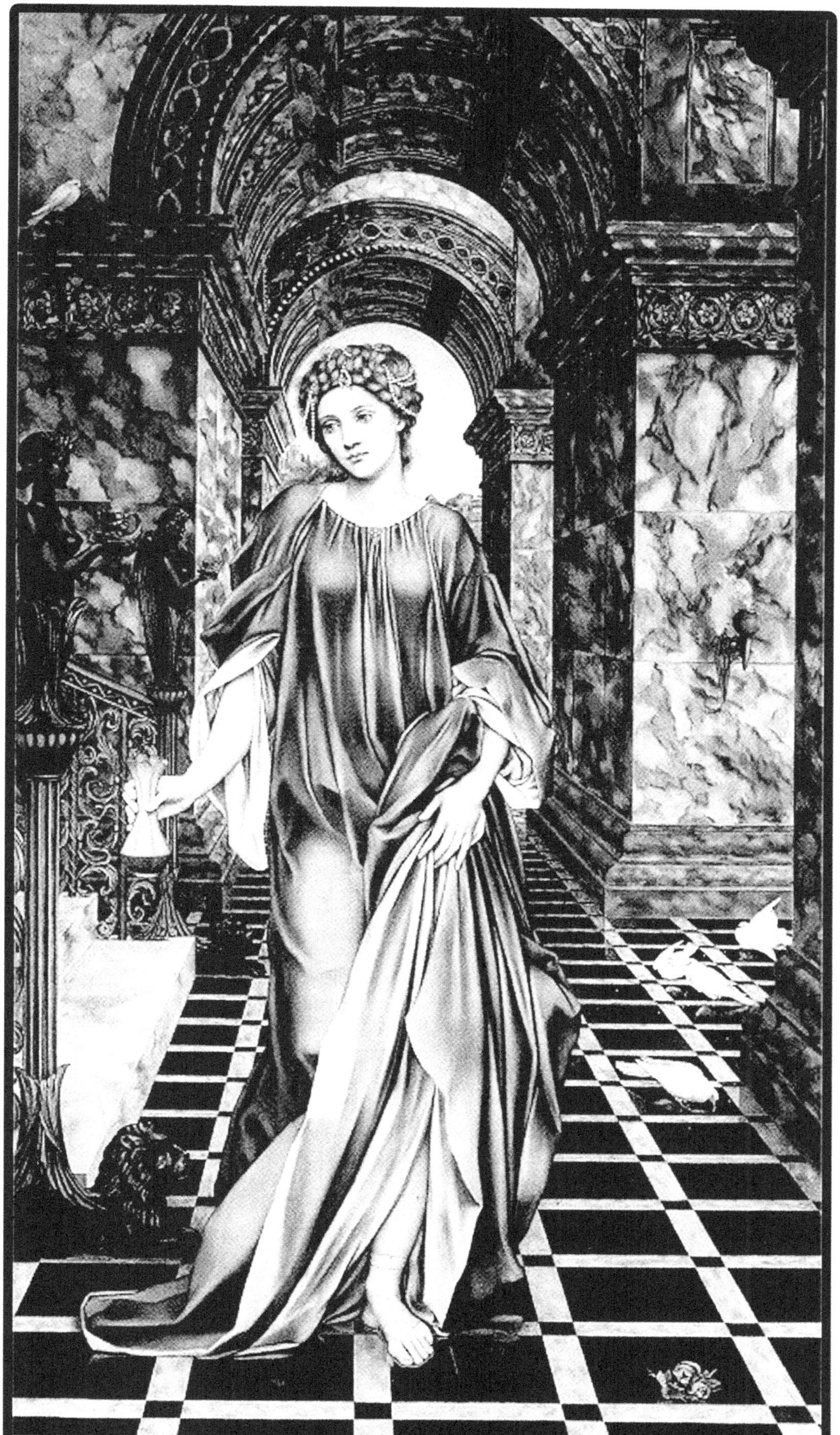

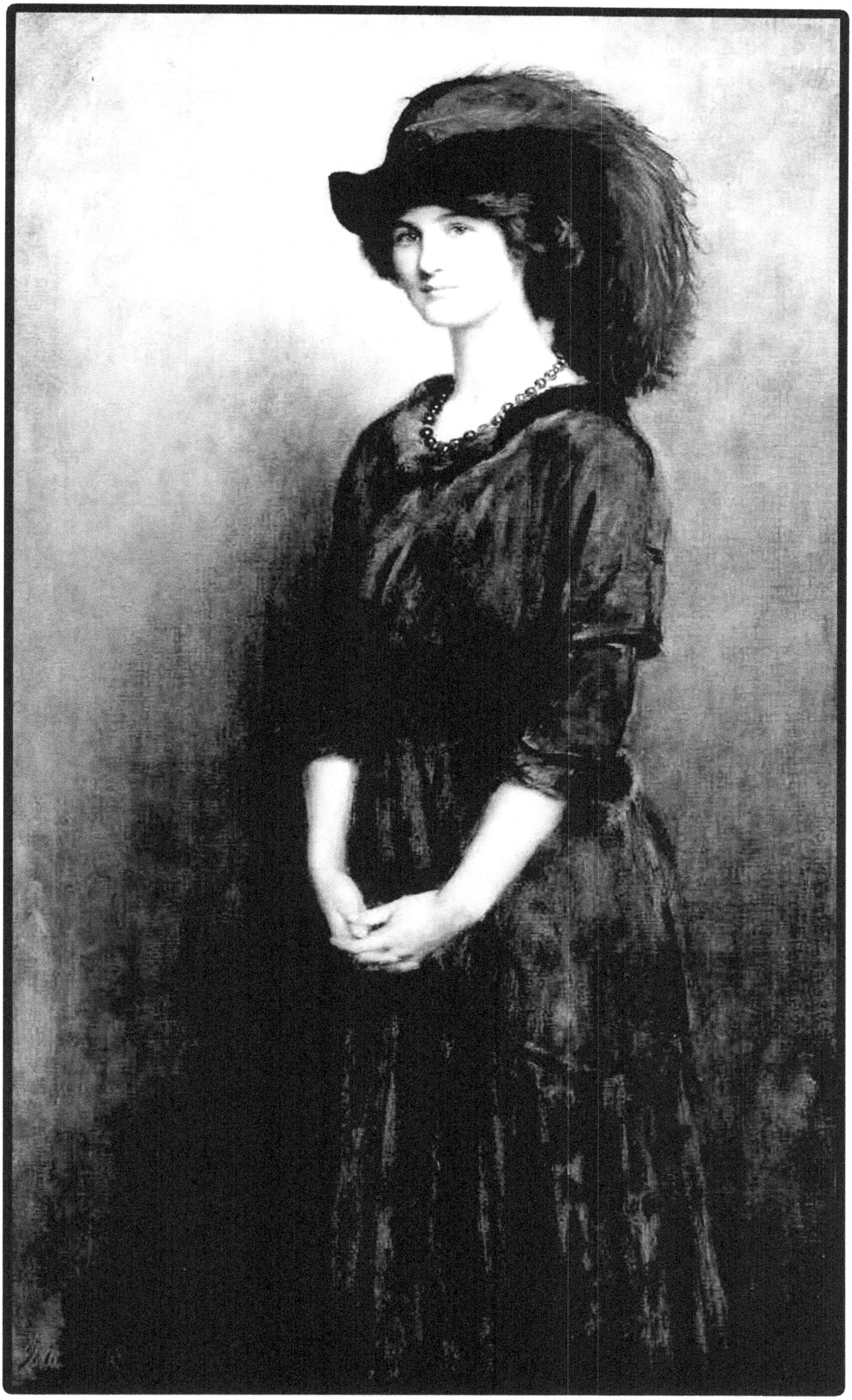

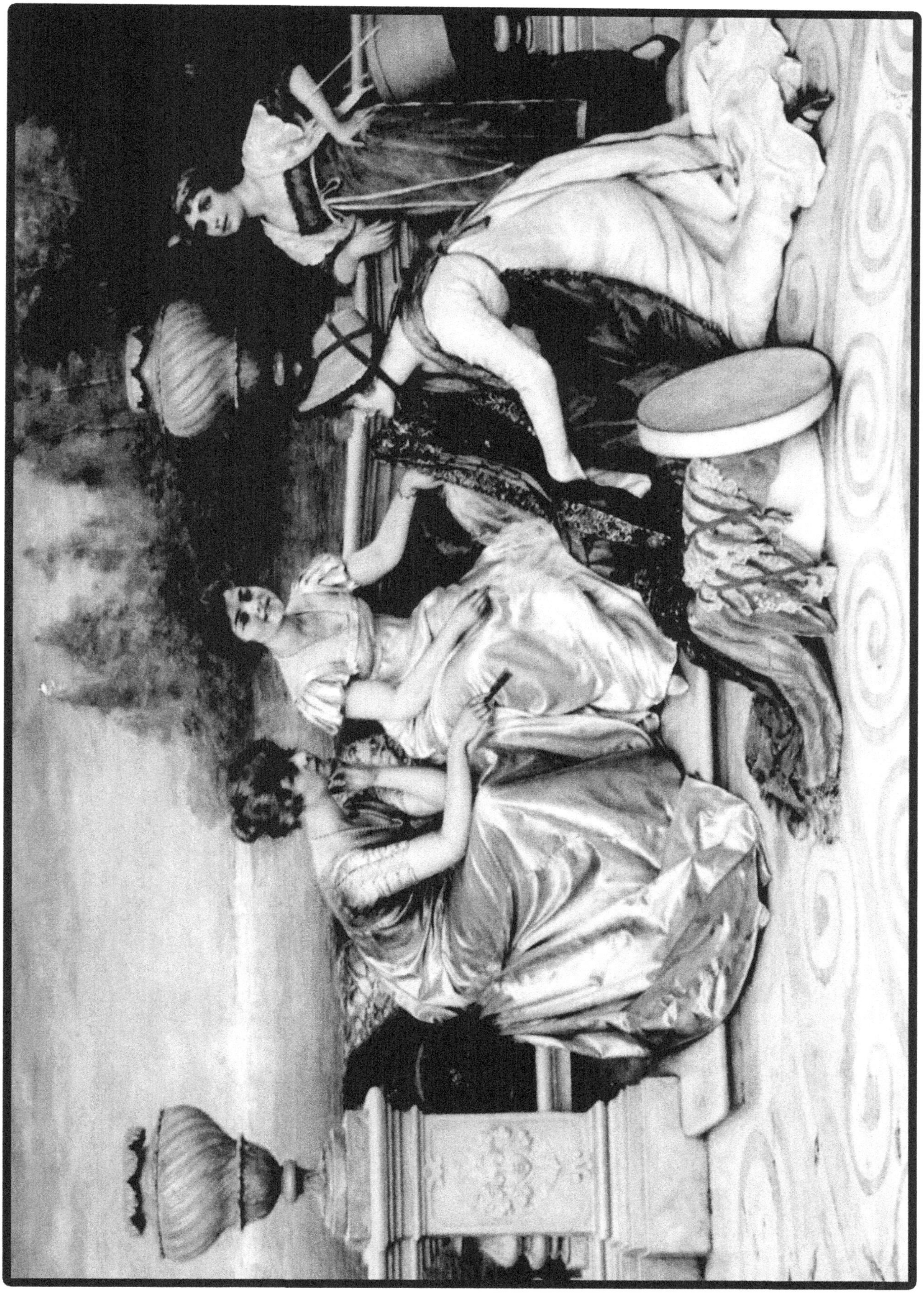

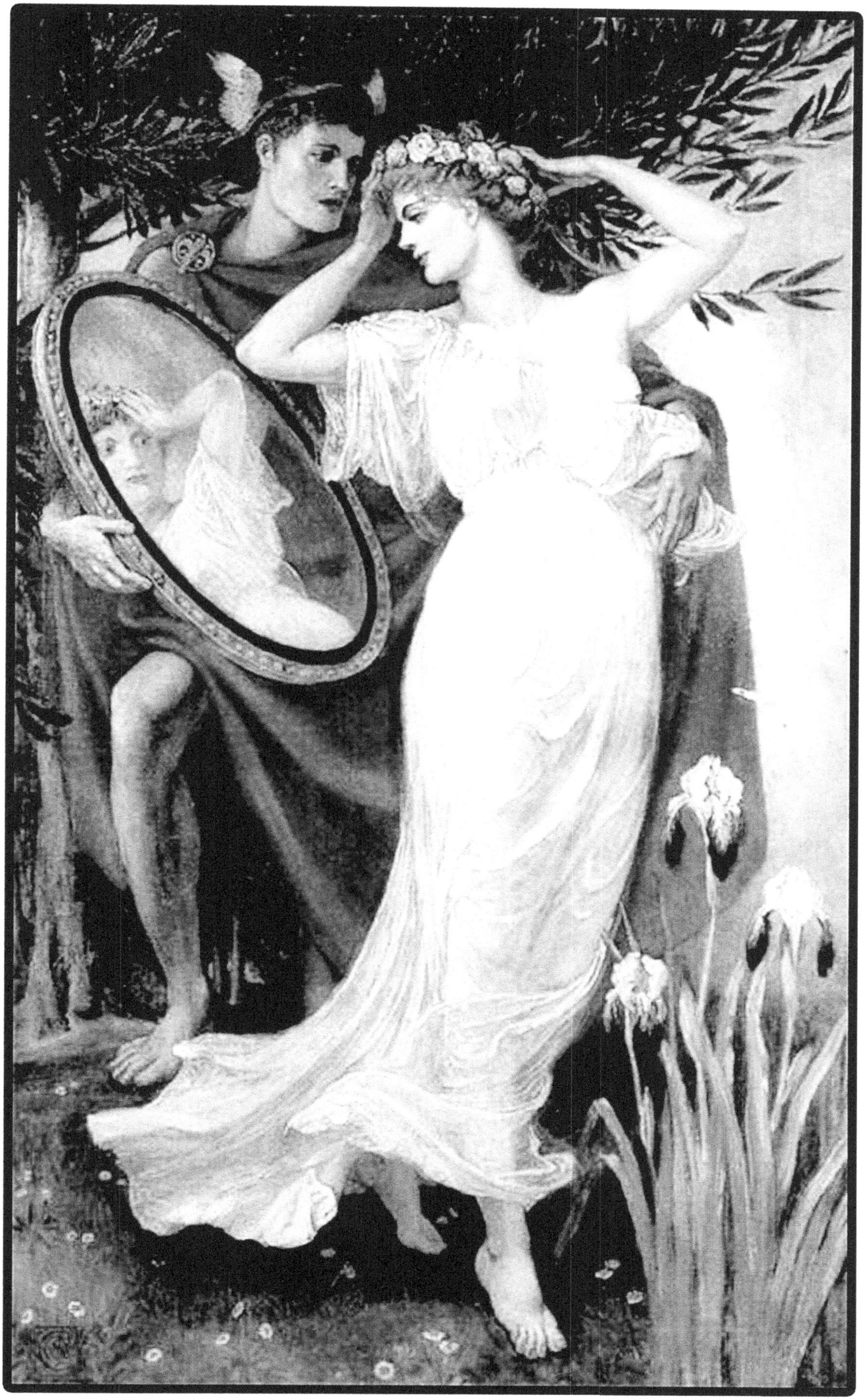

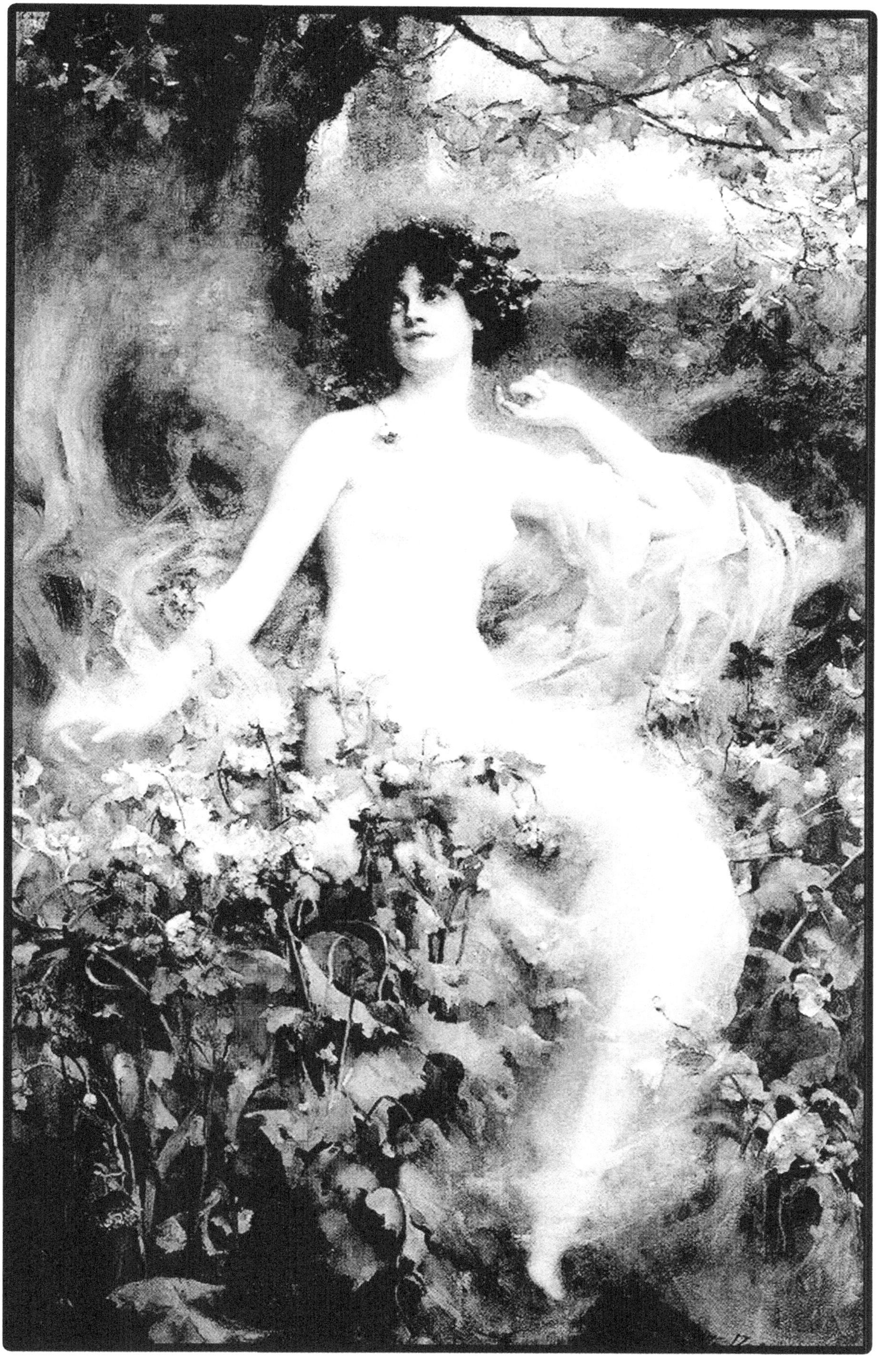

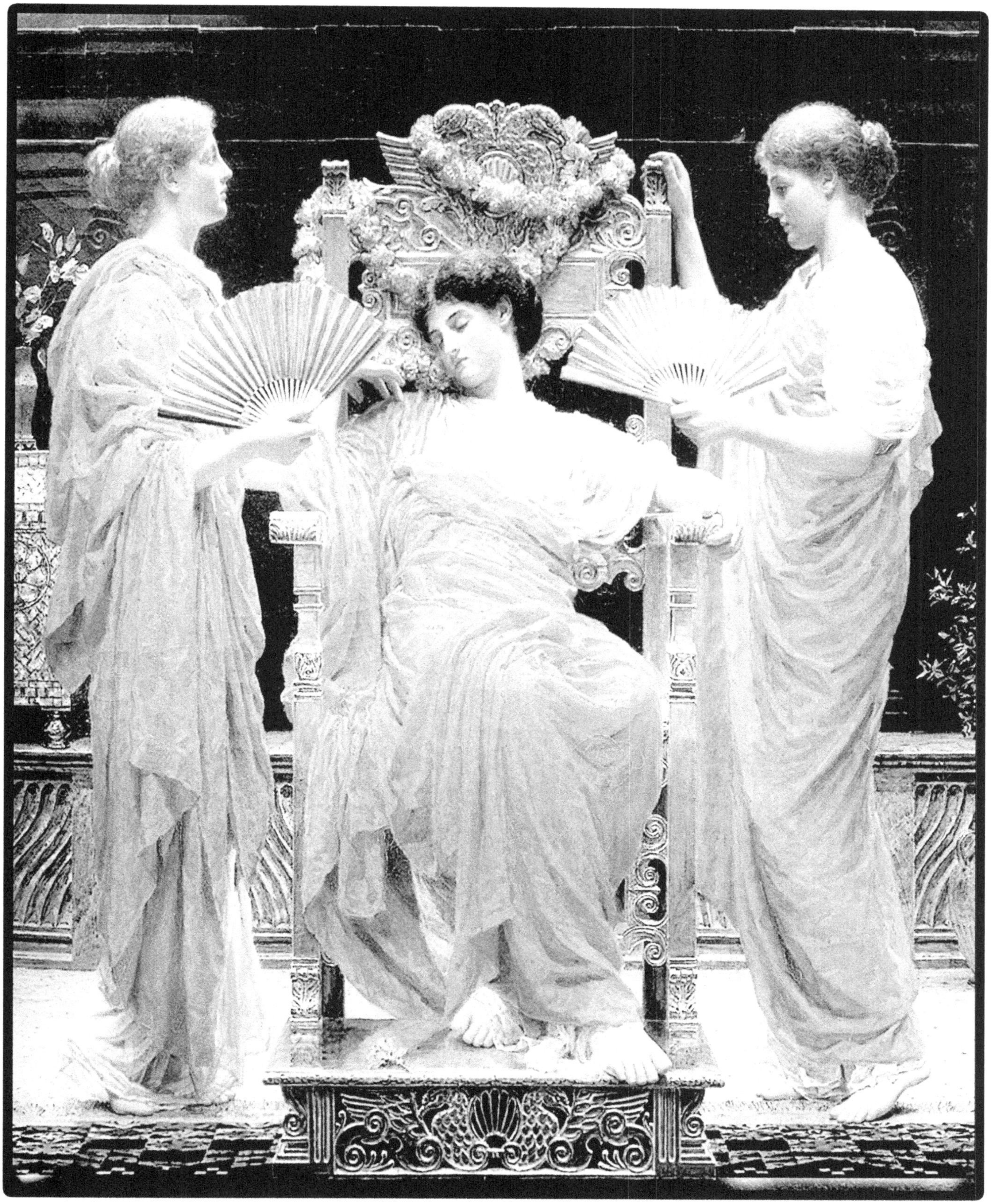

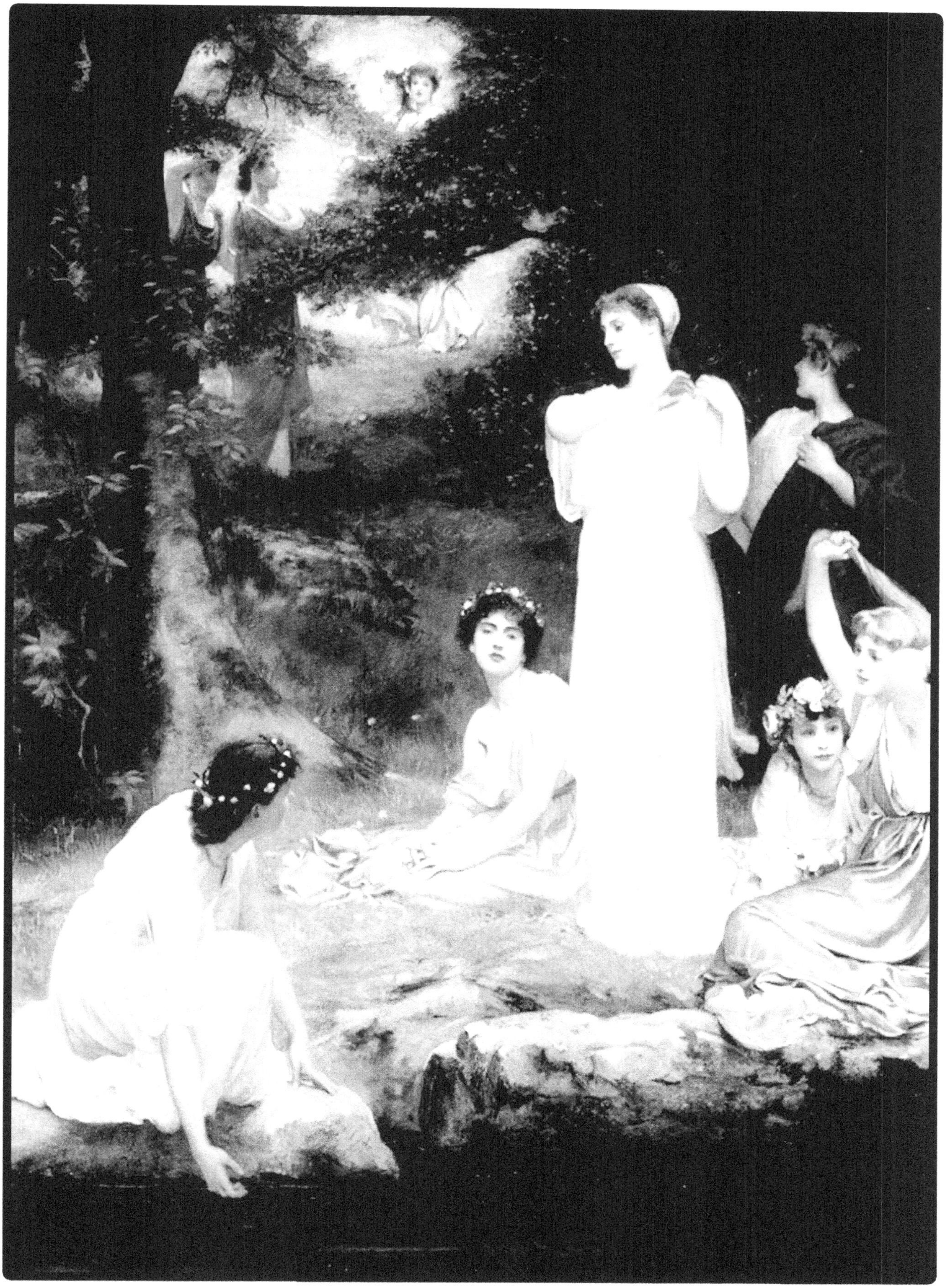

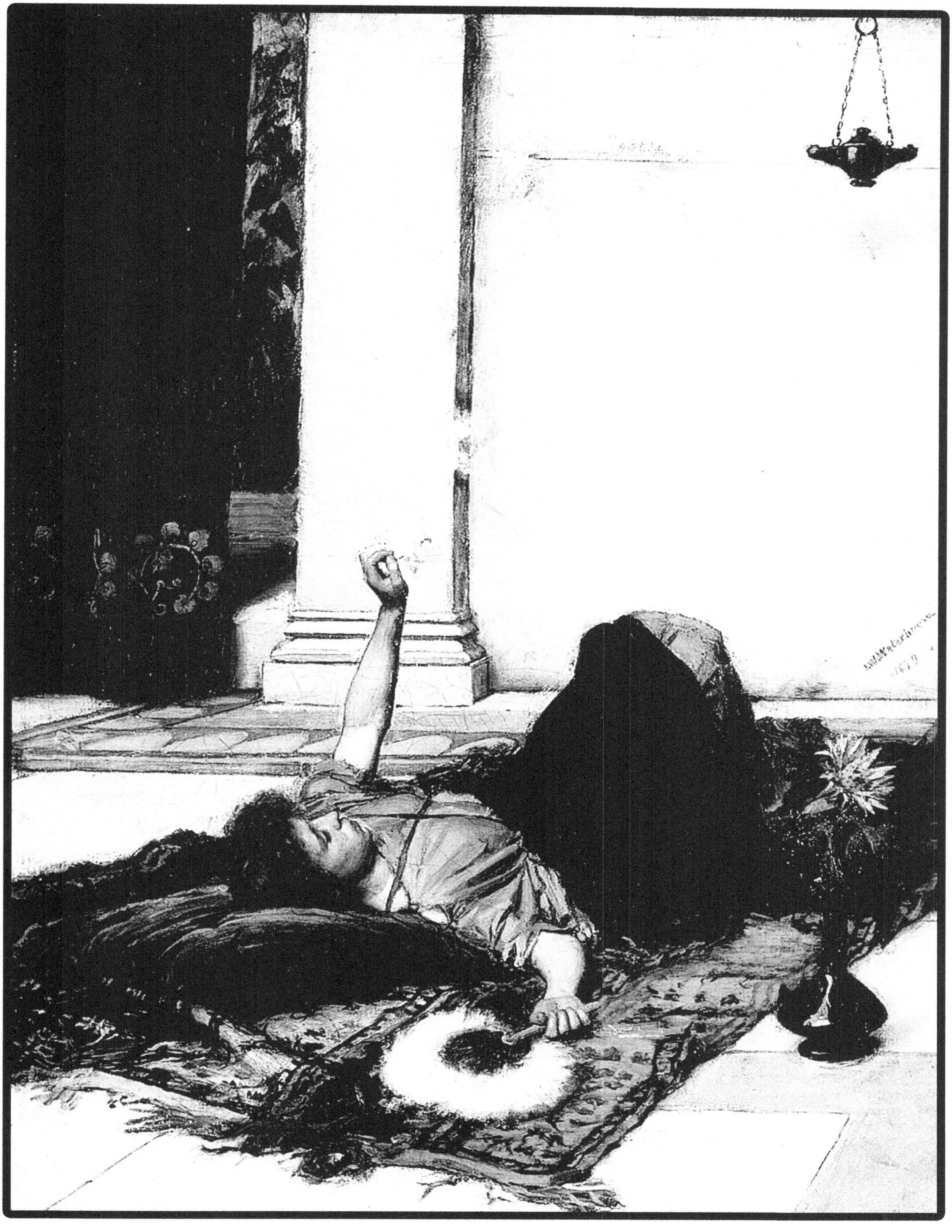

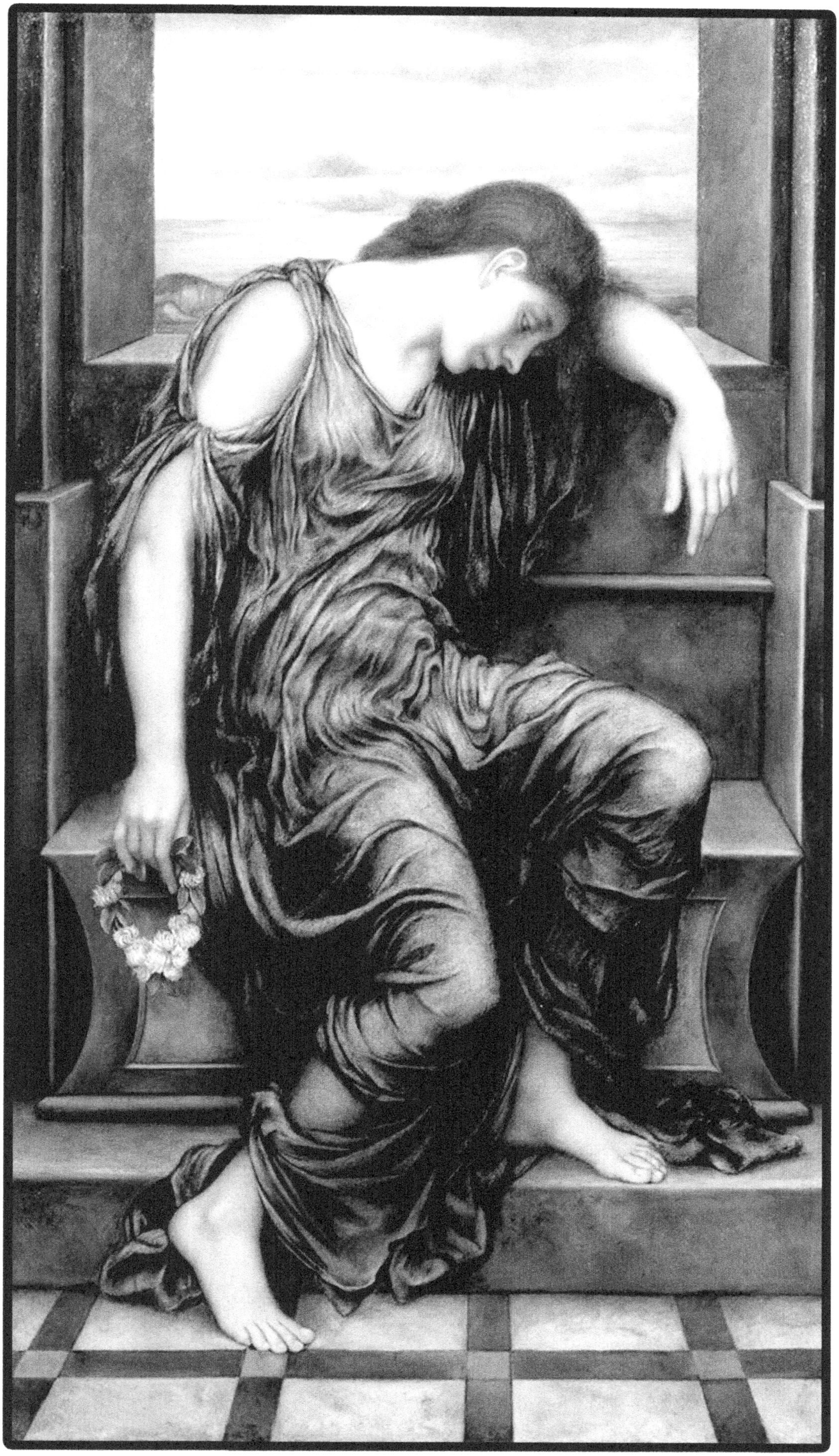

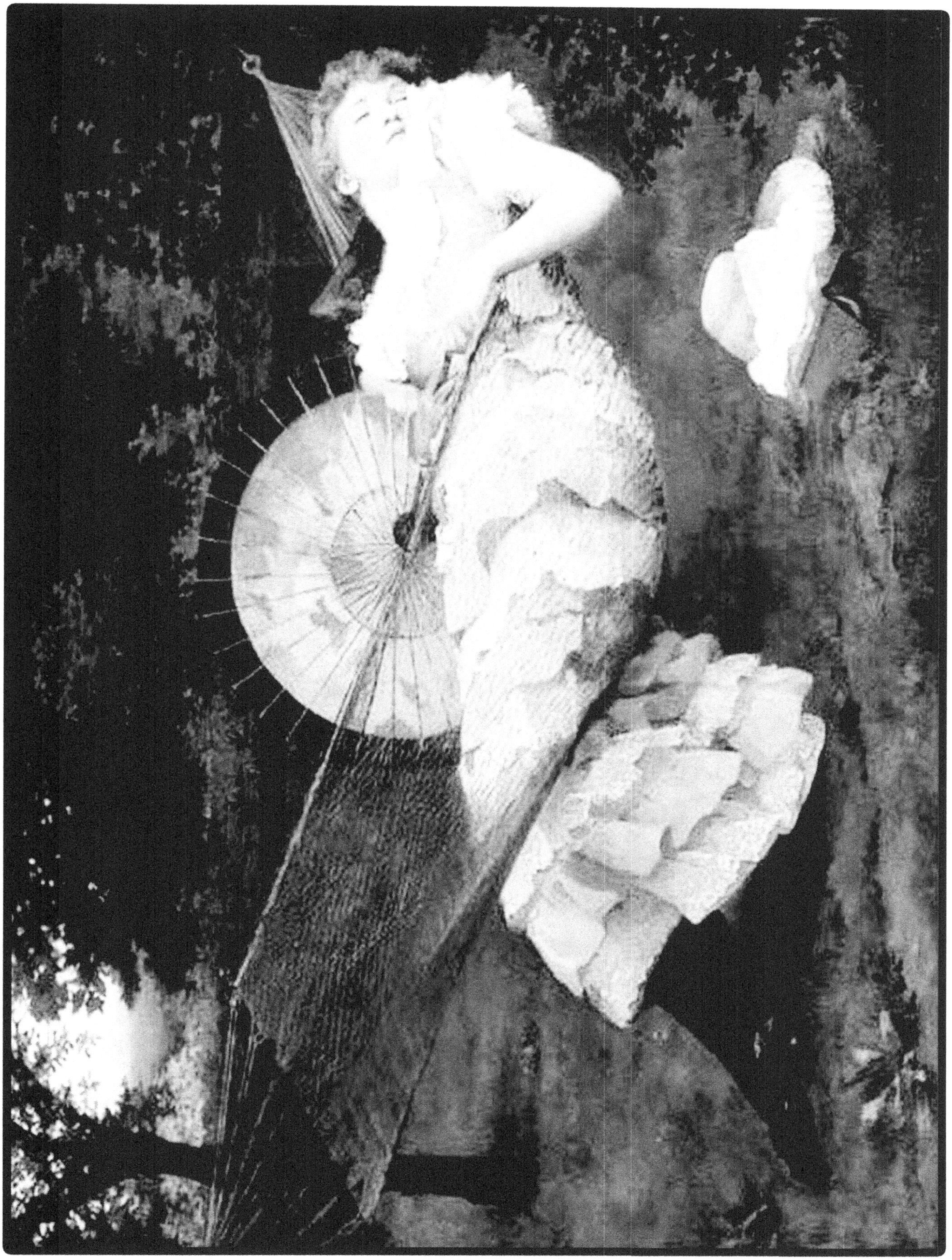

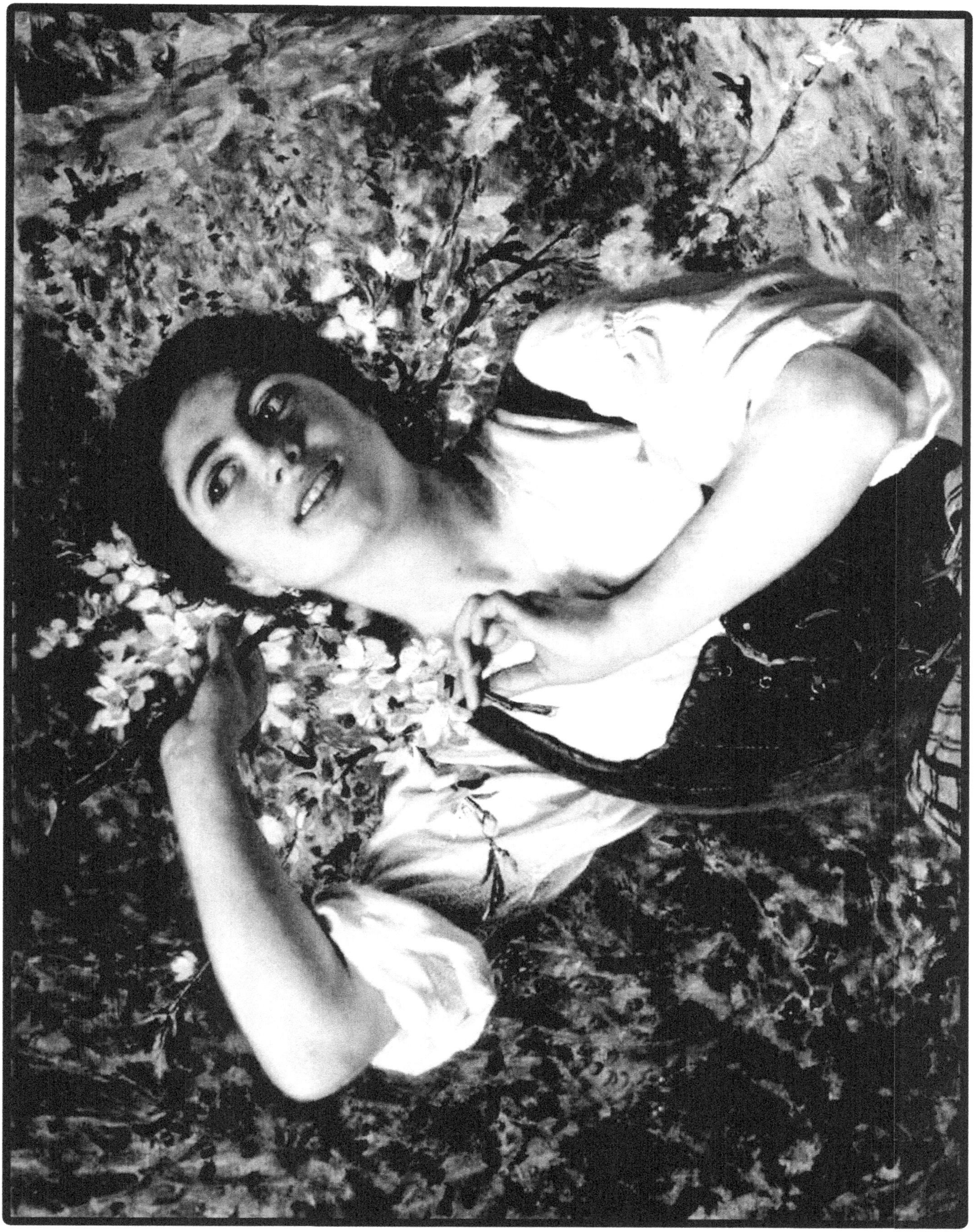

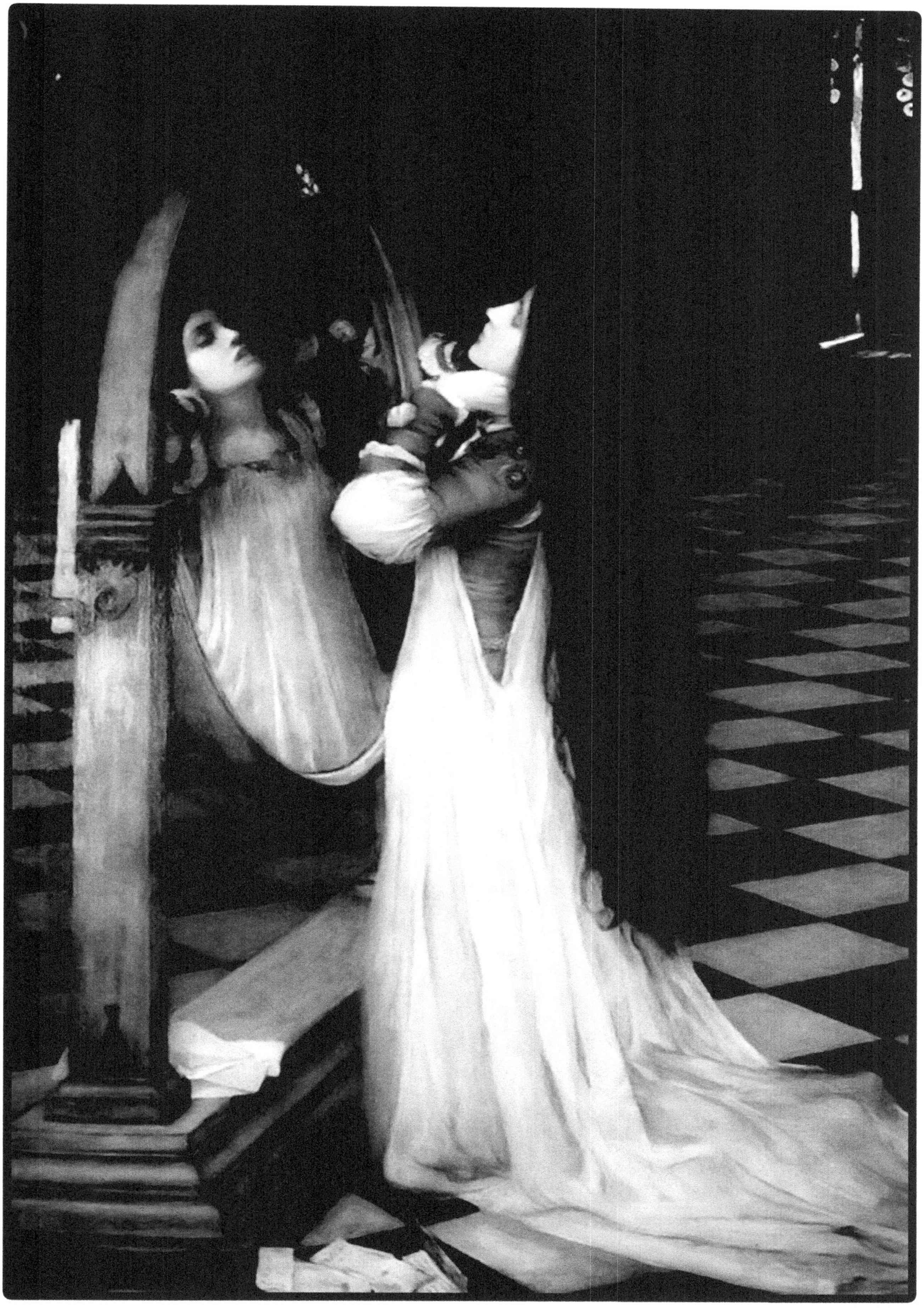

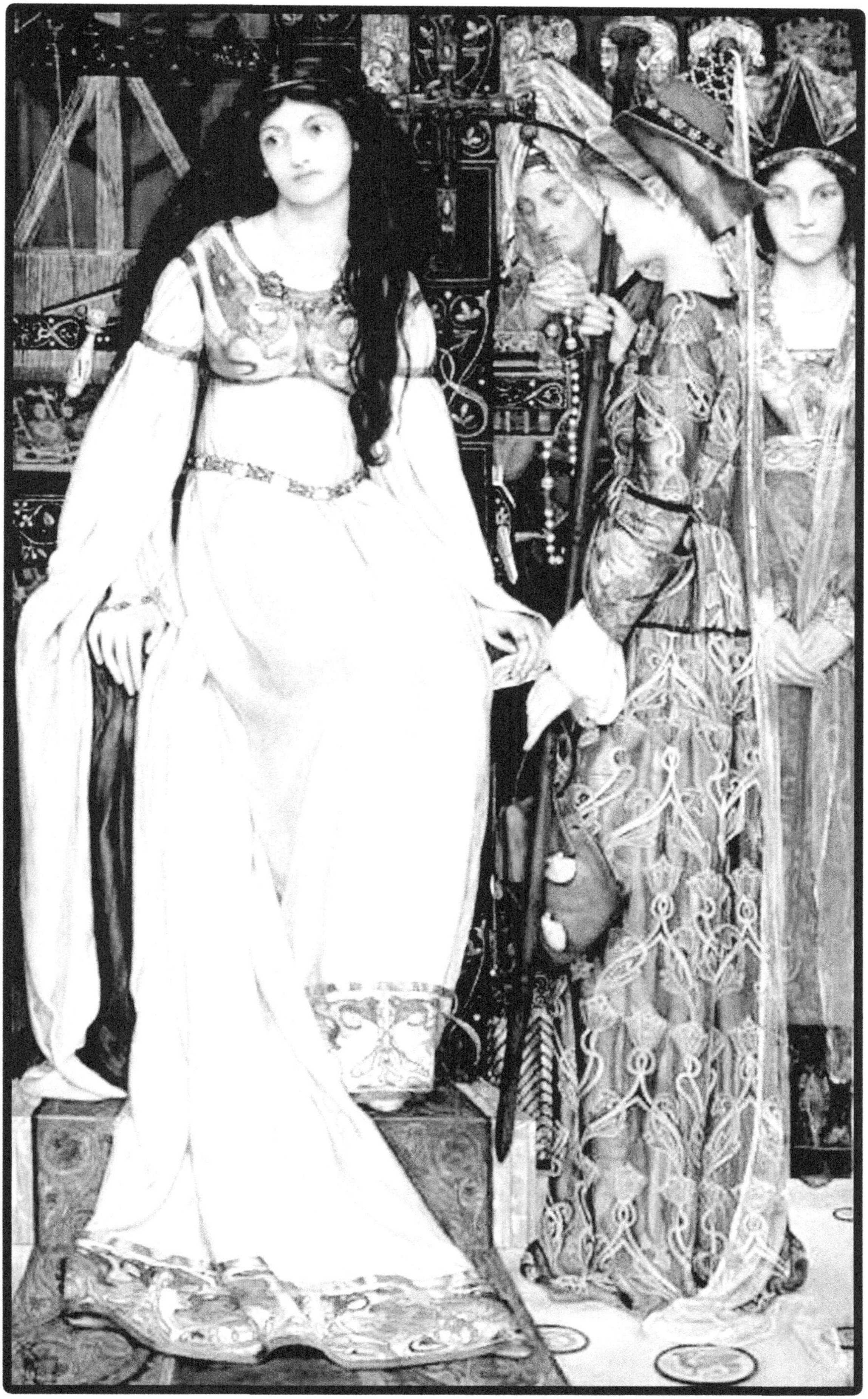

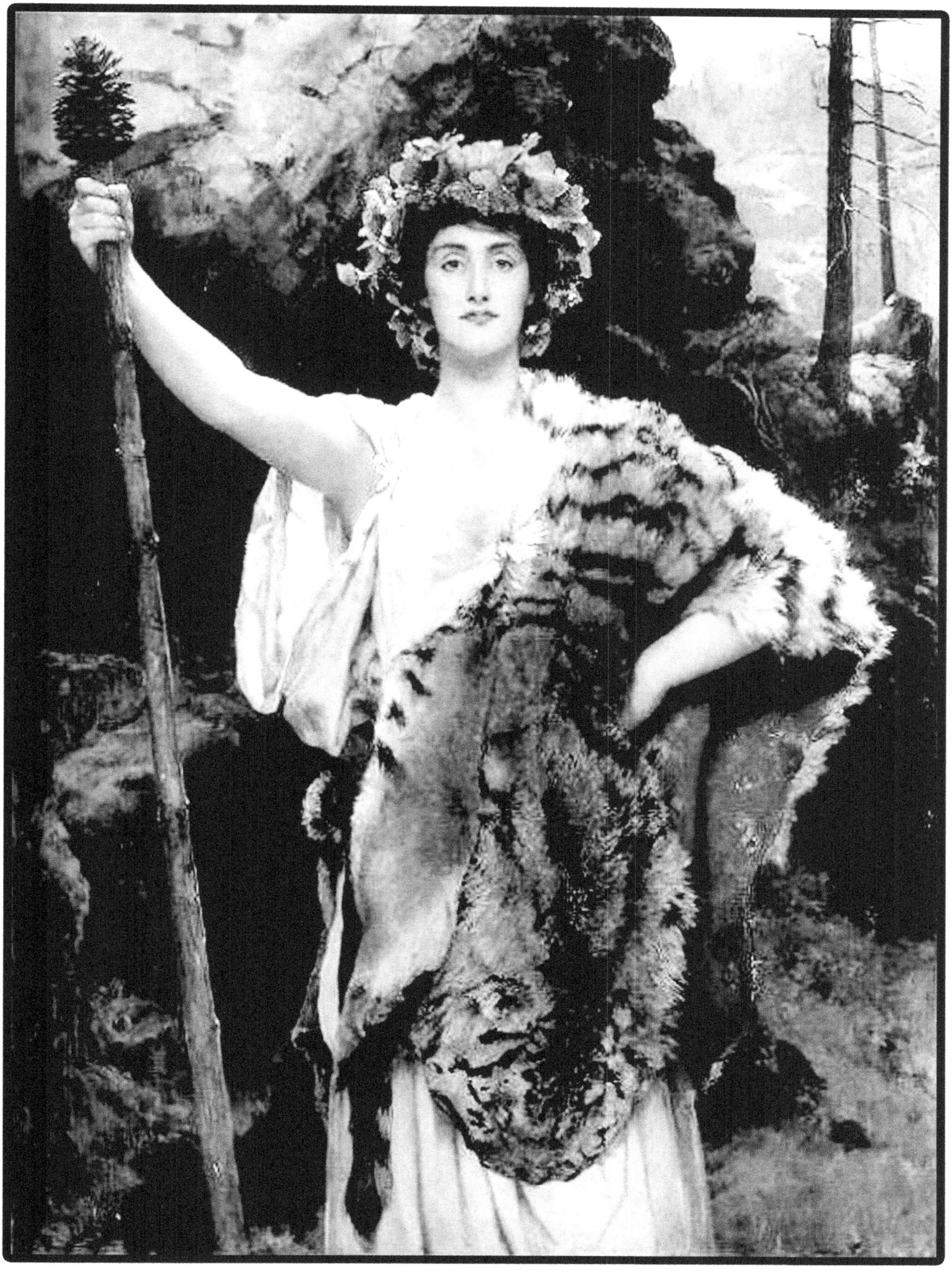

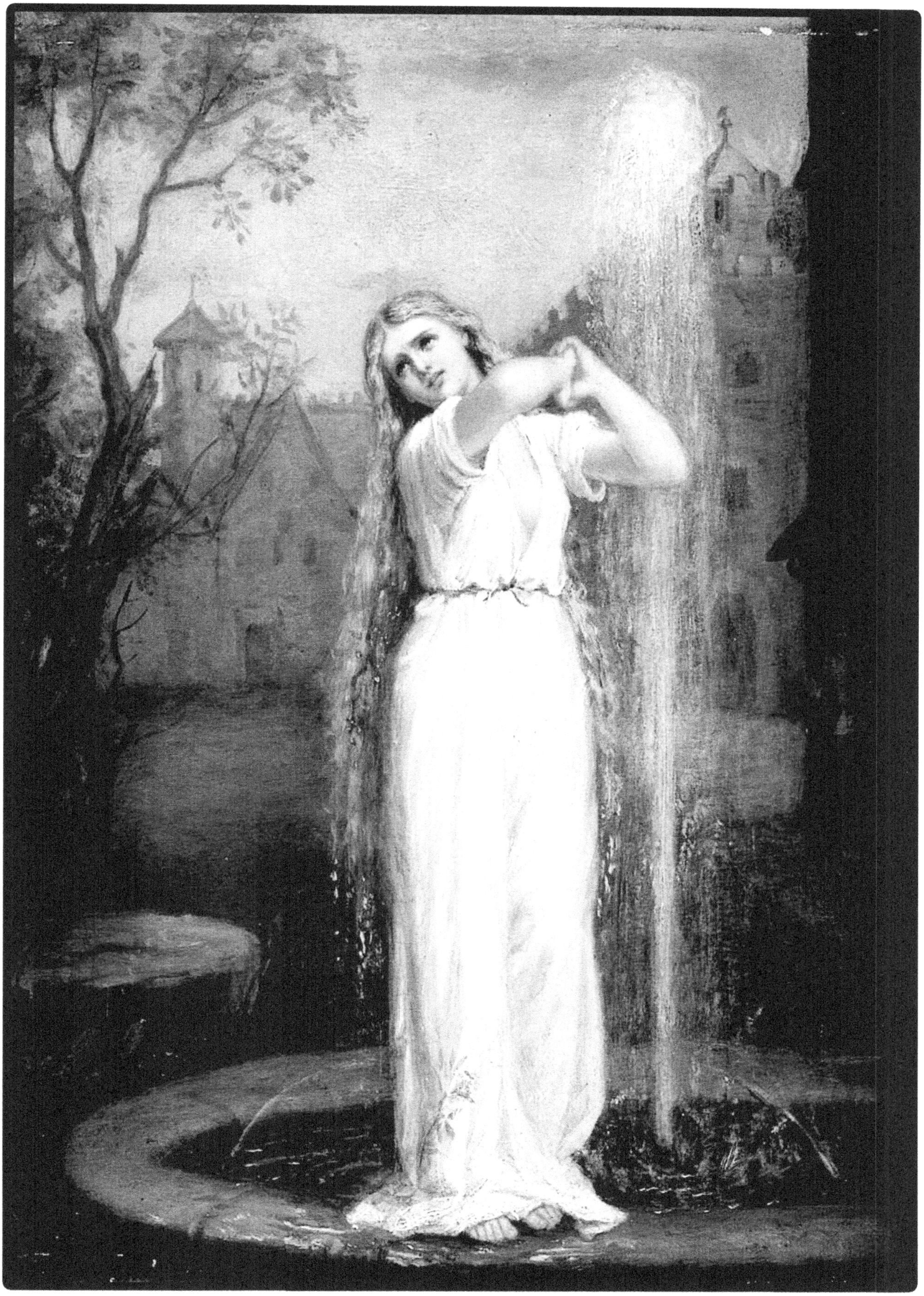

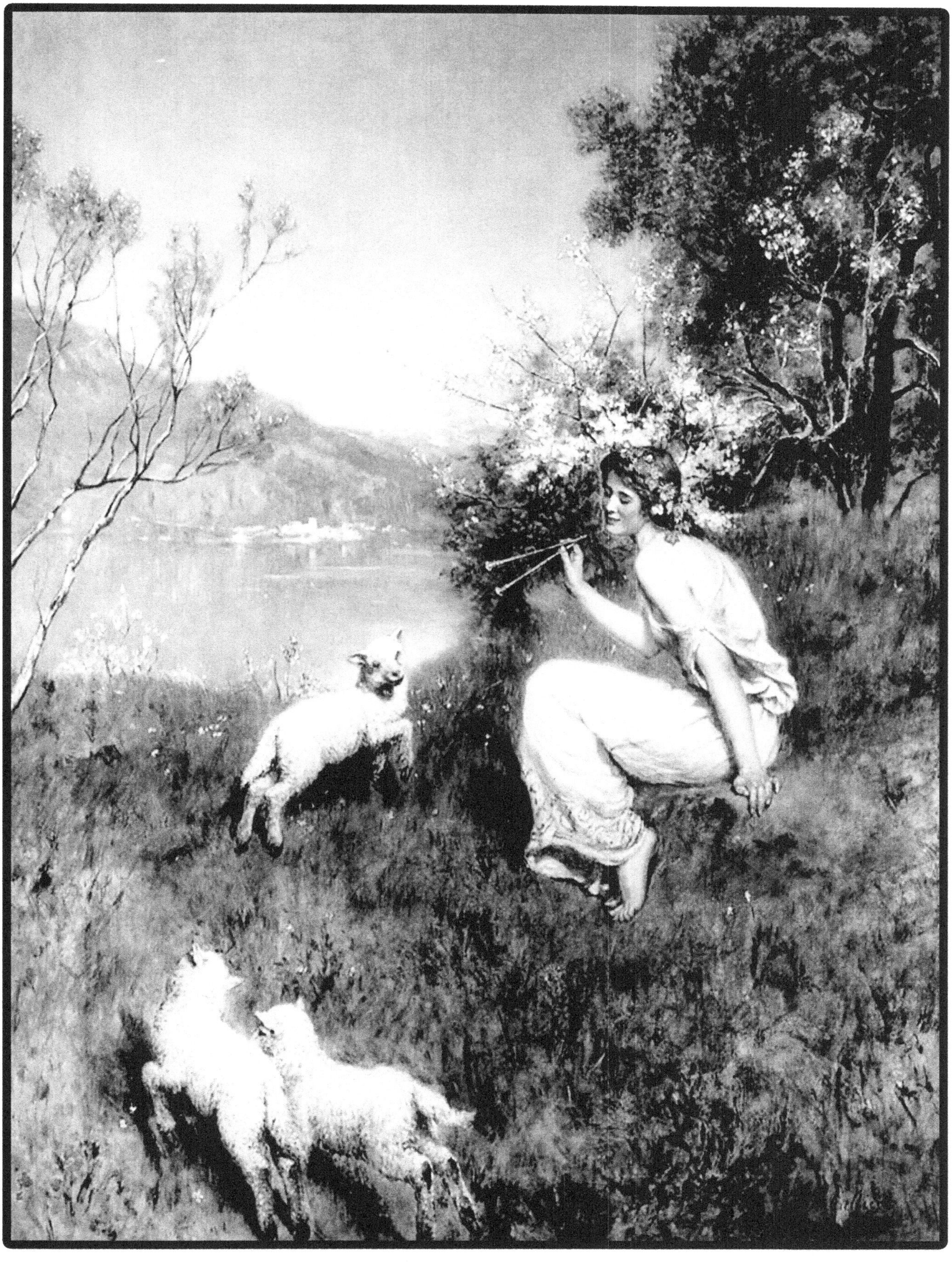

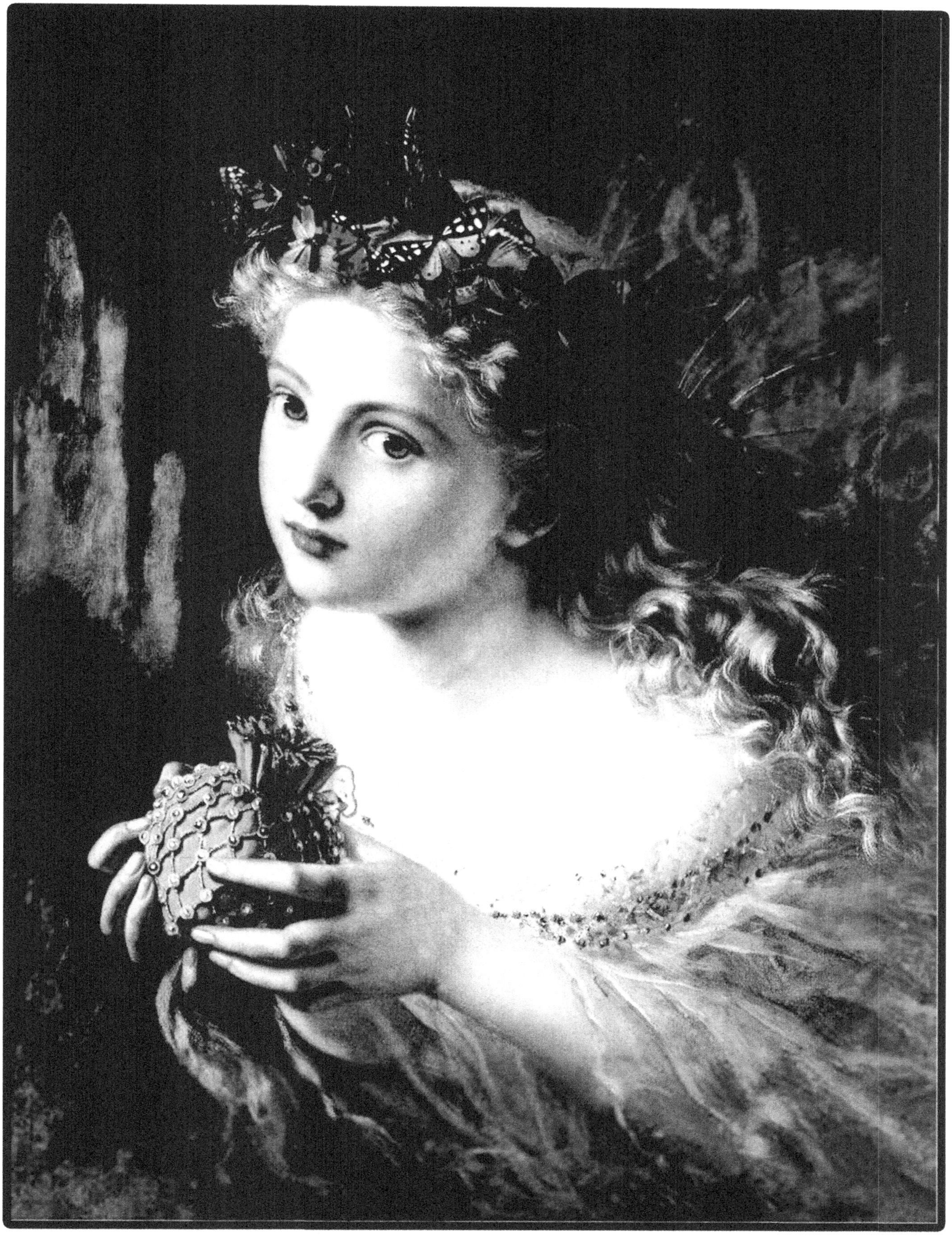

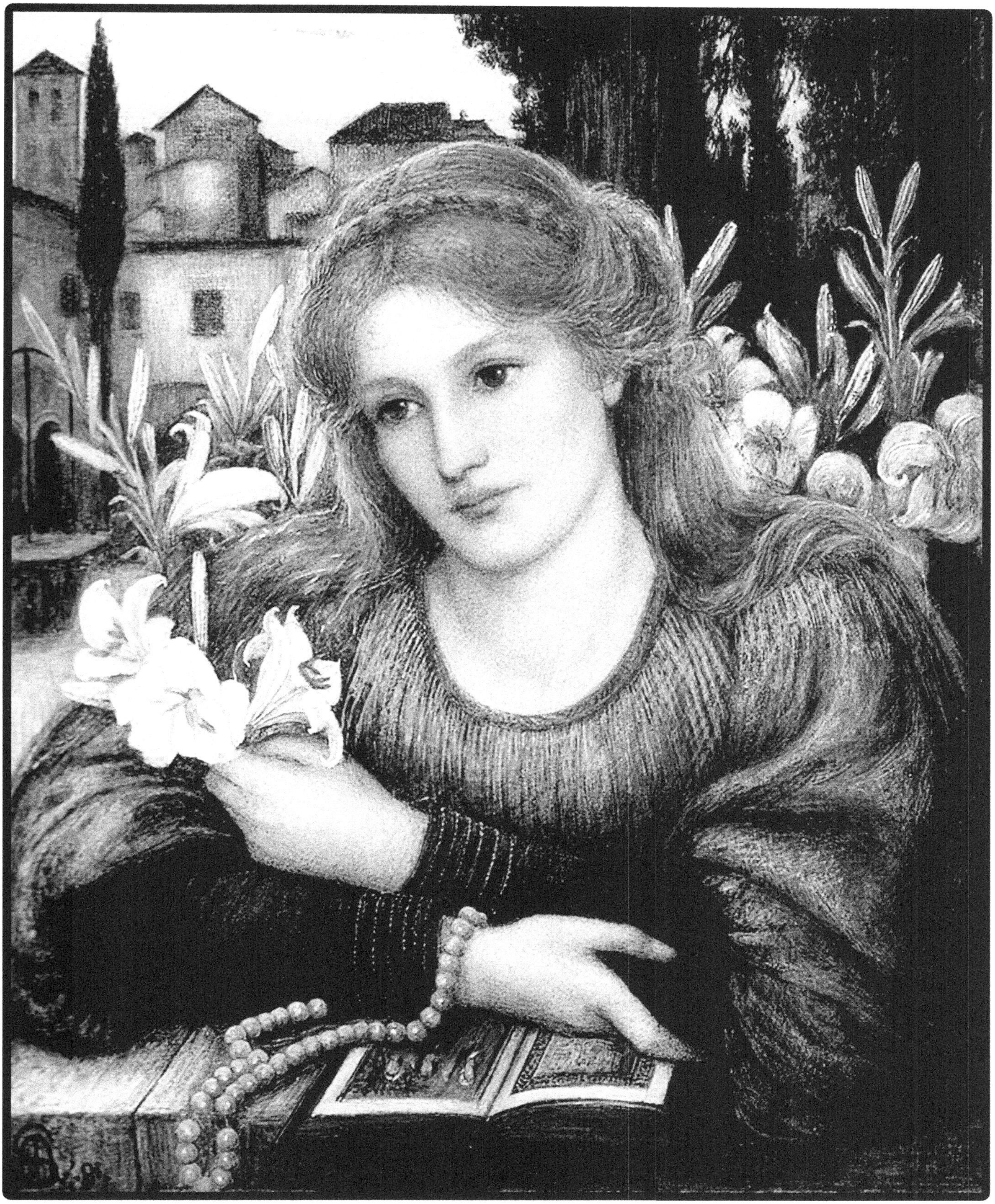

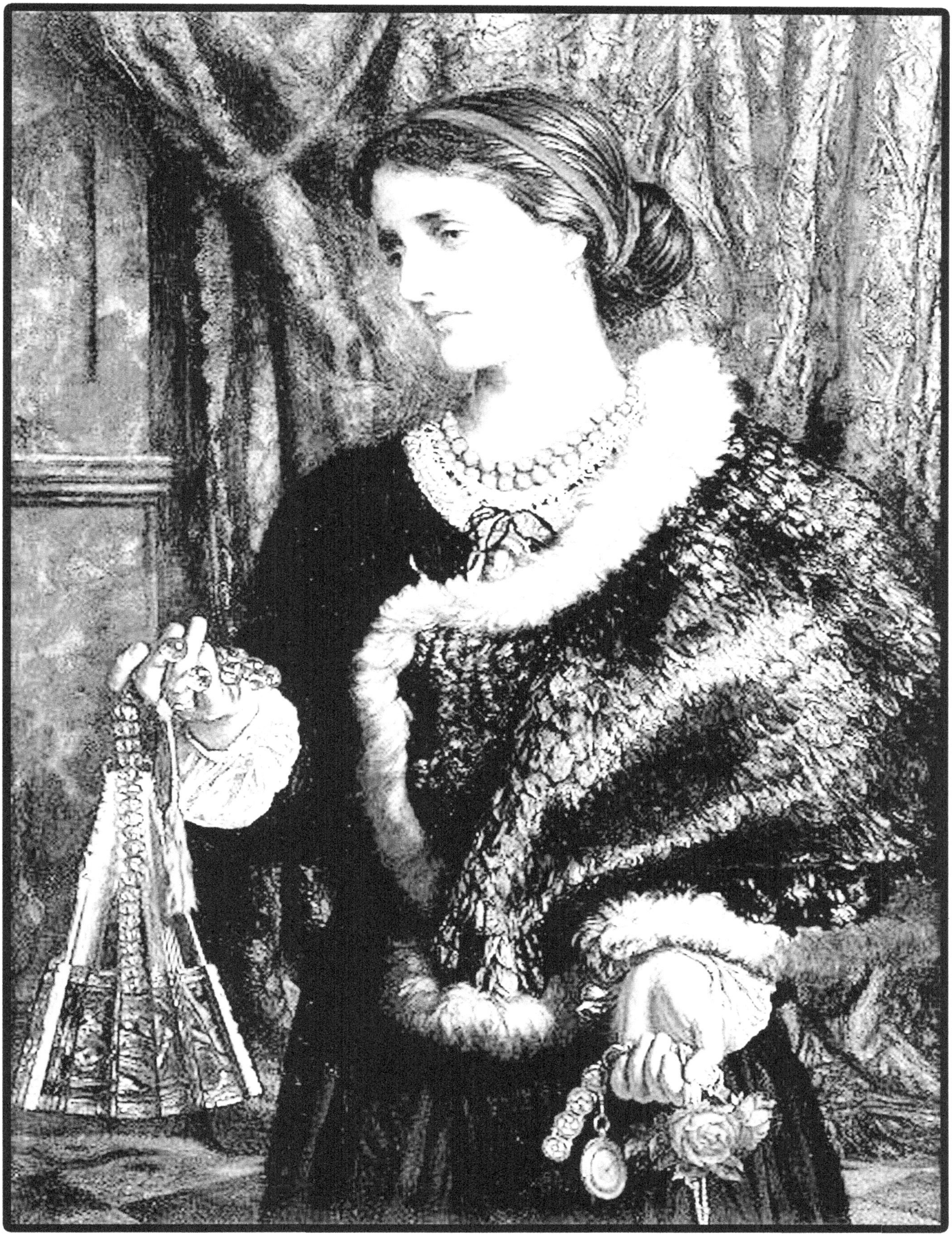

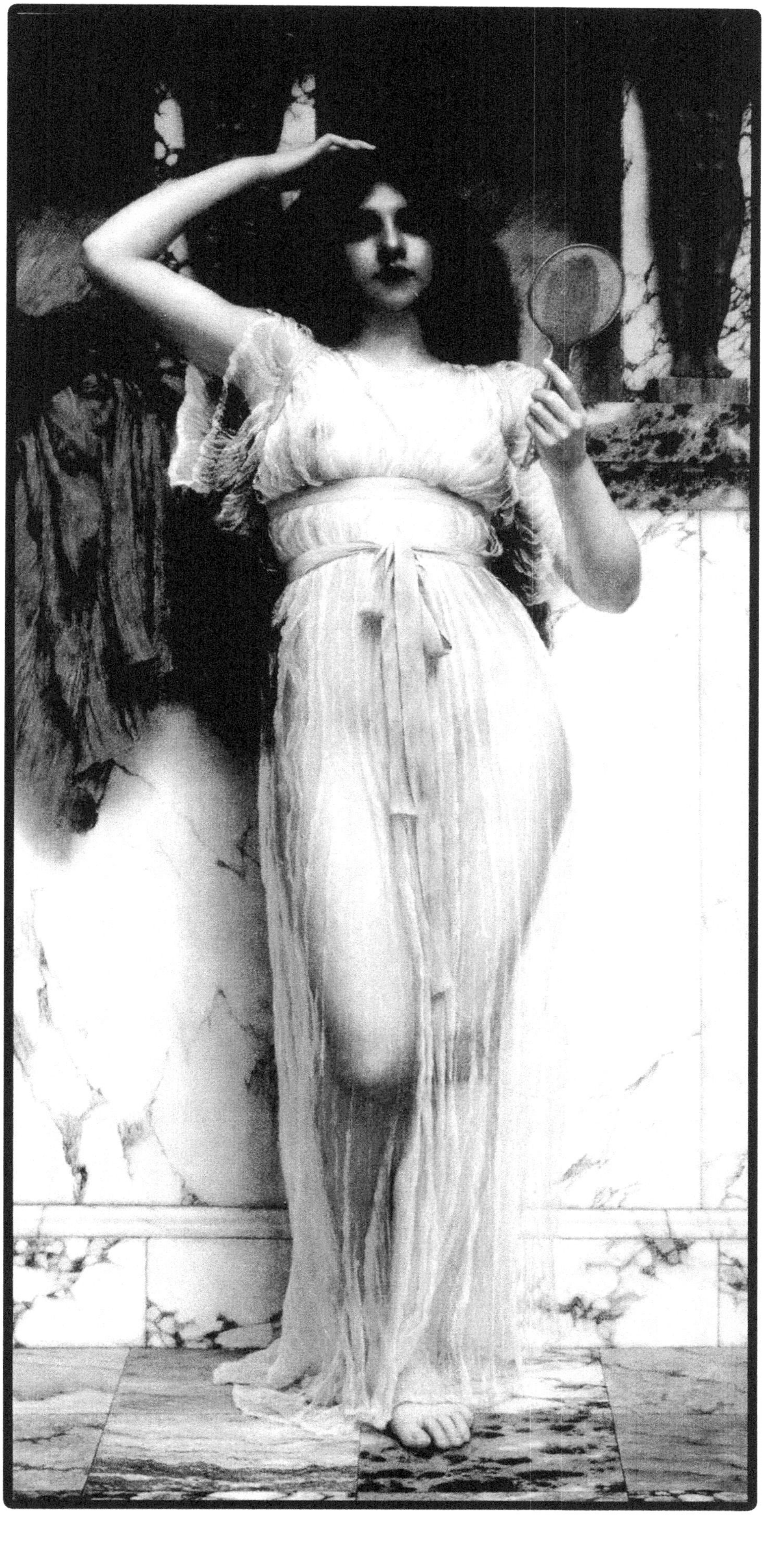

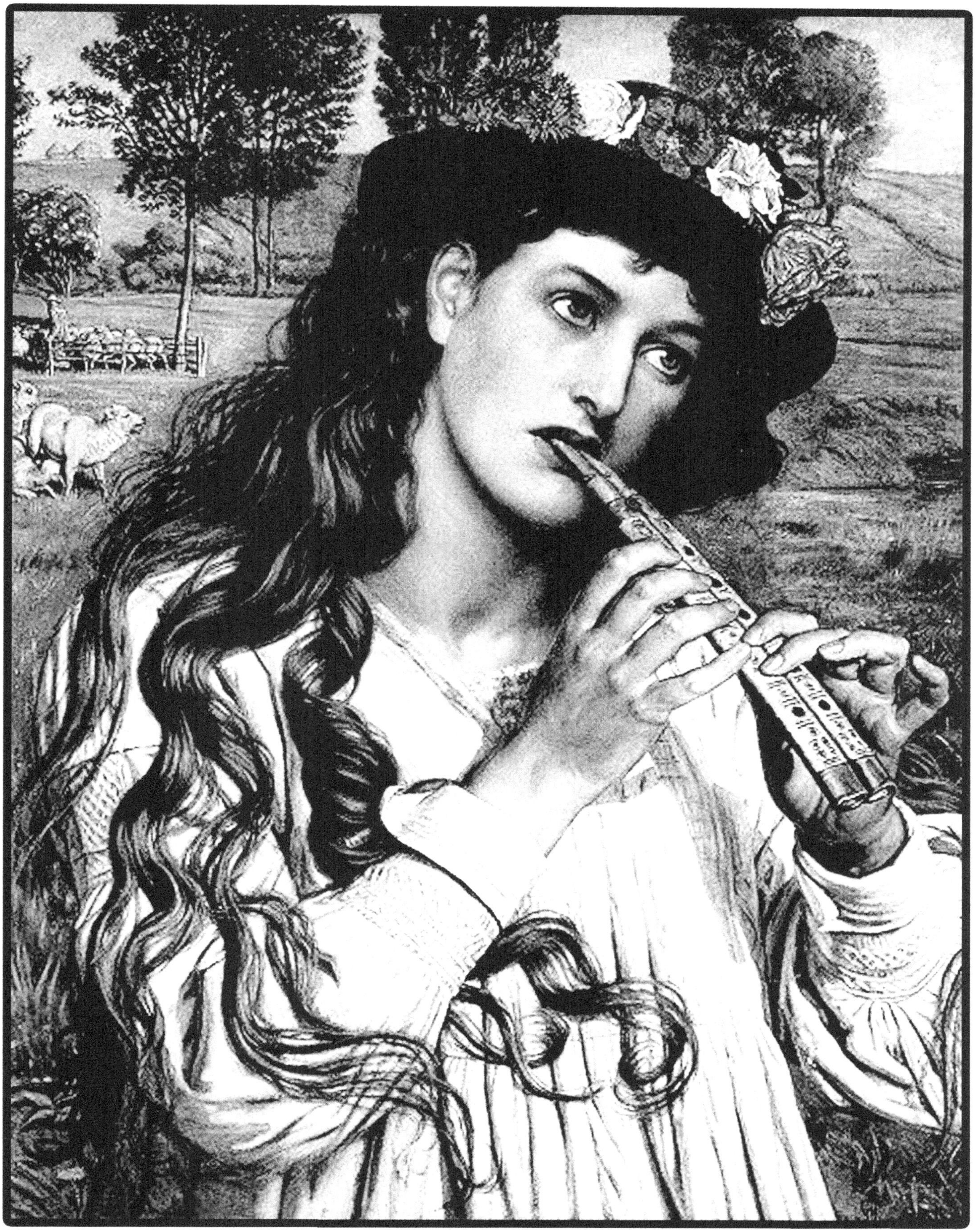

Made in the USA
Las Vegas, NV
22 January 2022

41614806R00033